Hero Dust

New and selected poems by
Tom Pickard

Allison and Busby
London

*First published
in Great Britain 1979 by
Allison and Busby Limited,
6a Noel Street, London W1V 3RB*

Copyright © Tom Pickard 1979

ISBN 0 85031 261 2 (paperback)
ISBN 0 85031 295 7 (hardback)

Set in 11 pt Plantin
and printed by The Bowering Press Ltd, Plymouth and London

Acknowledgements

High on the Walls was published by Fulcrum Press (London) in 1967 and reprinted in 1968.

The Order of Chance, Fulcrum Press, 1971. "The Devil's Destroying Angel" was first published in *Stand* and then in *Poetry of the Committed Individual*, edited by Jon Silkin, Victor Gollancz, 1973, and Penguin, 1973.

Dancing Under Fire was first published by Eric Mottram in *Poetry Review*, vol 61, no 4, 1971–72, then in an eliminated edition by Middle Earth Books (Philadelphia), 1973. It was first broadcast in 1975 on BBC Radio 3 (produced by Susana Capon), and its most recent appearance was in the Poetry Book Society's Poetry Supplement 1976, edited by Stuart Montgomery. Extracts have been printed in the Seventies and Leaping Poetry (edited by Robert Bly), *Vinduet* (Oslo), and it has been featured on BBC2 Television's "Full House".

1971–74 poems: some of these first appeared in *Poetry Review* (London), *Montemora* (New York), *Choice* (New York), *Hawaii Review*, *Lip* (Philadelphia), and *Contact* (Philadelphia).

The Jarrow March selection is taken from an hour-long programme of that title, commissioned and broadcast by BBC Radio 3 on 5 November 1976 (produced by Harry Catlin). "David Riley" was first published in the *Radio Times* of that week.

1974–78 poems: some of these have first appeared in BBC2 Television's "Second House" (produced by Tony Cash), *Smoke* (Liverpool), *Montemora* (New York), *Poetry Review*, *Poezja* (Warsaw), BBC2 Television's "Arena" (directed by Nigel Williams).

I would like to thank the Inner London Arts Association for the C. Day Lewis Fellowship, which I held from 1976–7 at Rutherford School (my thanks, too, to the staff and students there).

Thanks are also due to Alan Price and to Alan White, on the cover of whose solo album *Ramshackled* (Atlantic) the poem "Valentine" first appeared.

Tom Pickard is represented by Judy Daish Associates, Globe Theatre, Shaftesbury Avenue, London WC1.

Contents

This book is for
Joanna

Vis-à-vis Visa

this pattern
   we must learn
to live with
& love
each other

our days together
measured in advance
and stamped

but they
might learn
   from us
and soon
as we
   this day
delighted dance
our own
   and altogether
other tune

1962–67
from *High on the Walls*

High on the Walls

strange to be higher
than a bird   to watch them eat

when startled (the only
defence to be above)
take flight and land
at my feet

City Summer

summer to city dweller
means nowt but a change in the weather

sky
a mottled rock dove

            bluetits
            turn   burn in
            the wind

Cuthbert's Hut

grassplots laid with bricks
a roof of flimsy sticks
walls sunk
sky for the eye's
meditation

The Street Cleaner with his 18th Cent. Muck Cart

must have been used for "bring out your dead"
giant mexican hat wheels, no handles,
to be pushed along after the brush has done its job

and the wheels make the same sounds on the cobbles
an employee at the corporation yard but smiles
a flat cap a boiler suit but still that look
                              of the eighteenth century

you would say an idiot smile though I say old turnips
                    and blobs
in his cart with straw and broken glass are typical
he is his own man.

To My Unborn Child

our heads met
when both of us
bent to kiss
your mother's womb
you
little bairn
bent on opening it

and I pressing it closed
with my lips

then I found
you had been there
all time before me

The Bairn

you can't stop sleep, matthew
there's no shaking it off

each lash weighs a ton
and to keep apart
needs more than fun

pillows keep draughts off
as workmen leave geet gaps
in the cell

I tuck you in
your sweater's too small

twice tonight you've sneezed

"Puberty"
a painting by Edvard Munch

don't creep away from my cock
let's watch it grow
    let's sing songs
  to my cock
                and make your breasts bigger
            we'll unfold your arms
            and lie them akimbo

        uncross your legs
      and lie on the couch
        watch your hair sprout

The Bodies Are Touching

The bodies are touching
What is the matter?

Where is your mind now?
What does it matter?

Something is sleeping
where the mind wanders

It wanders away
Let the mind stray

It gives back a pain
It sucks and is suction

The bodies are touching
                    touching

Birthplace Bronchitis

The old men cannot walk up banks
without leaving brown *cockles* on the path.

They spend their days at pigeon duckets
watching *tumblers* and trains.

They're *on the sick*
and cannot leave their pain.

The thudding industrial hammer
is not much harder than the men it has made.

Our fathers are coughing up its grimy phlegm
and we will know the taste.

City Council Poem

The Lord Sheriff's gold chain
sparkles with the names
of hanged men

whose lifeless limbs
dangle and decorate his chins.

He has the honour to be present
at the scaffold
as his predecessors were.

Is it their heavy memory
which causes your official brow to bead?

Your sloppy mouth waters
at such entertaining deeds.

You said, when I asked you
what your powers were
that you could lock me up
if I caused some disturbance
in the town

but who, proud pig,
if you chose to knock me down
would lock you up?

The lead long drawn
from the mines
and the miners dead.

Their deserted workings
are left like monuments

where the crag crumbles
and the murmur turns
the stone to sand.

The ghostly trickle
of the stream
has washed away the silt

and a soul
poured into me.

The Game Bird

As I walked across the fells to Hangman's Hill
a family of partridge burst from my feet.
The young half flew, half ran.
Their mother feigned lame.

Returning, the same family flap
but this time for the fun of it
I chased the chick and caught her.

As I stroked her head she squeaked
and from the corner of my eye
I saw her mother lame again
to tempt me.

My hand open she dived for the heather
and vanished.
I would have brought her home for you
but feared her death
and your sorrow afterwards.

To My Friends Who Go

Remember the walls of this city
were built by you and me
we built ourselves a tower
and found we must break free.

Remember the city was vicious
the councillors greasy and fat
and the words which were in their mouths
had the nasty stench of cash.

Remember the dolemen and nabmen
are here and slimy as crap
look out for a lovely woman
but don't bring her back.

Remember we made more than money
we made something which couldn't be bought.
All it took was our friendship
nowt else to build our fort.

The Daylight Hours
a song for Dole Wallas

Aa hev gorra bairn
an aa hev gorra wife
an aa cannit see me bairn or wife
workin in the night

> *So go way Mr Doleman*
> *av got somethin else ti do*
> *than spen me daylight hours*
> *workin for you*

Yes aa am a song bird
and a song bird must sing
an you oh Mr Doleman
you'll not clip me wings

> *So go way Mr Doleman*
> *av got somethin else ti do*
> *than spen me daylight hours*
> *workin for you*

Grab ya job an ram it
in ya stupid gob
ad ratha gan ti prison
than de ya stinkin job

> *So go way Mr Doleman*
> *av got somethin else ti do*
> *than spen me daylight hours*
> *workin for you*

An if aa gan ti prison
the world will git ti na
the walls of a prison
isin strang enuff for wa

So grab ya job an ram it
in ya stupid gob
ad ratha gan ti prison
than de ya stinkin job.

The Devil's Destroying Angel Exploded

no sound
but horns of southern ships
and flapping wings

no colour
but dancing black

producers of heat
confused in the cold

moon full above the dole

sleep children of chilled night
whose fathers were black men
a miner's bright eye is no slave

sleep bairns
shivva now
ya fatha's gold is stolen

strong fathers of a harsh past
despondent now
slag faces rot against the dole

your hands held hammers
and demanded much
the moment passed
and bairns curled cad in the womb

worried troops and churches
you suffocated in the Durham bishop's stables
when Londonderry's jails were full

the coal you hewed
should have burnt them alive

instead you begged another shilling

beneath jagged brows
　　and stooped backs
making others rich with dust
　　which kills

you should have thrown it in their faces like a bomb
　　　　fed your children joyful stories of the blood of those
　　　　who cheat us

　　where we live
shattered smiles break
　　on haggard faces

manufacturers of filth
　　marry our wealth
in a confetti of votes

　　　　no breath of slum air

councillor elected by my father
　　he said you wore a worker's cap
called everybody *marra*
　　but the word I heard was slave

　　bloodfluke in the brain of an ant
that gold chain was scraped
　　from the lungs of pitmen

　　　　your gown is a union leader
gutted and reversed

　　　　look dozy fathers look
your masters have changed
drawn by the river mist
　　you drift in a dream

　　ah father your flesh is overrun with lice
and all your life you nurtured many parasites

Sleep

sleep explodes
deep inside us

my fingers
become butterflies

strange words
travel to my balls

sensual animals
move in a swarm
of warm sensations

My Daughter's Heart

my daughter's heart beats against me
gulls fly up river
white factory smoke flows east
still winter trees

grateful for the crows rough *caw*
so many sea birds circle the river
slow goods-train

movement in the still trees
stray thought starling
co-ordination of all things
in a moment

Death is an Owl

Death is an owl
that comes sweeping to me
she took nine months
to swell in the belly of her mother

On a clear night
I saw heaven
the star we inhabit

I called to God
for food for my family
my voice echoed in the alley
and the chill of winter
made me shiver

Going in the World

as I was running up
the down escalator
I passed Jeff Nuttall
running down the up

For Spike

when you see demons
open your eyes
blow out the smoke

Mr Mostpeople's Message to Me

"everything is marketable
souls are old hat
besides we've got them
all in the bag

ideas or objects
concepts or things
poets and even poetry

you invent it
we sell it
you become it
we project it

[your reaction to this bulletin
has already been sold]

impressions our speciality
provided they're as flimsy
as the other clouds of shit
with which we coat the people's minds

leave them in peace
let the people sleep"

New Body

As you saw my leopard's coat
I was a tiger

As you felt my bear's claw
I was a snake

As you stroked my cat's fur
I was a fish

As you built me a lion's cage
I was a worm

As you gripped mountains
I was a stream

As you crept tunnels
I was the sun

As you sought warmth
I was snow

As you expected thunder
I was calm

As you expected blood
I was stone

As you expected shape
I was air

As you looked
I was invisible

As you felt
I was near

When I appear
you tremble

The Order of Chance

entered a strange monastery
the order of chance
observing plants
how they grew
vision being nourishment
amply feeding shape
and turning leaves

eye in restless head
catches glimpse
of twisting leaves
green flames/frozen

watch it grow
           stand years
stand cold

does it move when I sleep

passing glances are enough
        growing on the fragile stems of plants

1971
Dancing Under Fire

Dancing Under Fire

love is just
love is just
love is just
a pile of dust

a narrow bridge
leads to a ruined castle
protected by wolves

a miner carved in stone
above his tomb
green
and black only now

taken from the roman wall
to build instead of defend

to construct towers

others used one slab
at a time
to represent themselves

a blue fish
gave me your address
showed uncharted land
lay between us

flowers obstructed us
butterflies clung to our eyes

walls were dissolved
one after the other
as we grew closer

owls of dissent
hovering only to preserve that space
between us

you were a dream
as I approached
withdrew

someone said
the instructions
were not meant
to be read

and understood

blackbird flew
to top of
sun tip
tree

all
below
became dark
he sang

how the *master race*
longs to be enslaved
in the bedroom

slave
secured in his dream

hard
no wind
nothing changes step

love
flesh and faith
alone

see my own stone stances

one fixed gaze
burns into life

drums beat
a retreat to the stars

a sinking flaming head
quenched in the darkness
throws light on the cycle
light dark light

      holes drilled into city concrete
      to fill with concrete
      no crack uncovered
      no gasp of green

      a graveyard
      gives a splash
      of living colour

      the victors thirst
      for their own more terrifying defeat

      what taxation and energy
      is required to maintain it

      how the people
      beat their guns
      into chains

      she

points out the attic window
to a dragon coiled
in the valley

tells me
street lamps mark the roads

and the roads
are old

I ask for words
and her hair ignites

brings in
the dragon

I ask for a lance
she shows me bracken

to kindle its fire

red
& dancing

black
& burning

>   *her*
>   *eyes*
>
>   the soil we squeeze
>   makes coal
>   to give the fire
>   the wings we need
>   to fly
>
>   we shuffle through you mother
>   to our deaths
>   took our claws to build a nest
>   and whisper to each other
>
>   we've grown wings and fly together
>   leaving you the woven twig
>   that shaped the egg

dragons flame
a local call to the sun

once kept firmly beneath the turf
men and boys
went below the surface to revive you

blistering whore made us wolves
and I like the rest danced round
ancestor burning

out of their tombs
out of the rock
into the air

tall lady in the dark corner
take off your hat
we're in possession of a dragon
and he lights the room with fire

wind blows through
the windows
flicks the trees

glittering of stars

tonight we travel the passageways
and tunnels
all is dark and warm

movement
becomes peace

curled in my stomach
burn with flames
that give no light

little black flame
in my little black belly
little black flame
in your own black belly

I am the dark
do not look to me for light

the train rumbles
in the valley

dream of dragons
roaring in my belly

look through eyes of darkness
and discover darkness

the voice that speaks
is clear
my own
falters

whose head
is this
I gnaw
to a bone?

secure and sealed off
in my womb
answer one word

cannibal   cannibal   cannibal

what flesh there is
is yours

cannibal   cannibal   cannibal

that hand you feel is yours
those words are yours
the air you breathe is yours
the walls you touch are yours
and impenetrable
shaped into a shell
windows of darkness
walls of darkness
your teeth cannot crack rock
doors of darkness
leading into darkness

sleeping sun
a pea skin your strength

the only nourishment
your swollen tongue

eat that   and stay alive another hour
but lose the power of speech

c

dissolve dissolve
reduce to cotton wool
and still dissolve

reduce to white sea-foam
and still dissolve

dissolve to fishes in the sea
and still dissolve

dissolve to eggs beneath the leaf
and still dissolve

dissolve to fibres in the roots
and still dissolve

dissolve into a fish's eye
and still dissolve

dissolve into a sea-gull's beak
and still dissolve

dissolve into a sea-gull's crap
and still dissolve

dissolve into the salt within the sea
and still dissolve

dissolve into a spot of blood
and still dissolve

dissolve into a kiss
and still dissolve

dissolve into a tongue
and still dissolve

dissolve into a lick
and still dissolve

dissolve into a mirror's eye
and still dissolve

dissolve into your own desire
and still dissolve

dissolve into her warmest fur
and still dissolve

dissolve into her breast of milk
and still dissolve

dissolve into your sucking lips
and still dissolve

dissolve into the air
and still dissolve

the milk burns in your throat

the flame is yours
you are the flame

the river's voice
is many-flamed

*

Always shook. Always trembled. Always walked, Marta from
Westerhope. We called him Marta, and he always shook. They
said he was shell-shocked. No one knew him. He always turned
up. Sometimes twice or three times a day. No day was
complete without Marta. We thought he was a spy, or wanka.
Wore a slouch hat and rain coat in all weather. *If yi gan ti
Kenton Woods, Marta'l getcha Marta'l getcha!* The more we dis-
covered of the world outside, there was Marta. He was no joke.
Silence when he passed. Great stories followed him. Hero!
Raper! All the time his fingers trembled, his eyes blinked, pull-
ing a hat over his face. *Watch out for Marta!* Got red hair and
walks all day. The large world must seem small to Marta. A
hush round the lamp-post when he passed into the next lamp's
light. *Hoo here's Marta looka!* Tall and thin. Speaks to no one.
A ghost from another age with bombs and trenches. Mustard
gas and Marta. Steel helmets and Marta. Bayonets and Marta.
Medals and Marta.

one two three
one two three
marta'l getcha
on is kneee

four five six
four five six
marta'l tek
down ya nix

seven eight nine
seven eight nine
martaz name is
frank en stein

Tot from the shop said a bomb exploded in his trench. Comes in every day for his Woodies and matches. He has no words. Only demands and memories of old commands.

marta's got a blade
in his mack
marta wears an old
gas mask

marta got a shock
in the war
marta he can't fuck
anymore

marta's got no cock
in his pants
left it on the shores
of france

He wasn't anybody's husband. Not that we knew. He lived somewhere else. No one knew. Motherless Marta. Left her with his enemies and memories in the trench. Similer to Himiler only he's never been in the Albert Hall and his balls were used as anchors for his cock to stop it floating off like a zeppelin every time it sniffed fresh air. Marta oh Marta your lack of words makes us suppose so much. Do you get your dole on fridays?

a train replaces the dragon
roars in the valley
engines shunt

a voice from someone's telly

oh you watch me
on the box
my lips move
my eyes are dots
my tune is an electrical cackle

wired magic
in a wooden box
I am a coffin
with a window

you can watch
see me flicker
if you touch
I will shock

it's not electric
interference
that makes me present
shadows
of the real event

I am rich
I am greedy
pay the rent
and I will give you
anything I invent

my hand to her breast
tore away the cloth
as her foot touched my leg
ran over a field scattering birds
smelt the damp grass
blood to a gallop
peewits flash their white bellies
my finger tips exploded at her tits
a rabbit dashed to the stream
gull white and wisely perched on a bridge
cocked its eye at a fish

her nipple filled my mouth
implored me to relax
whisper silver fishes in her ear

one touch could crumble

edvard munch's soul
stirs in her womb

with no glib intent
lay my head on her belly

she licks my ears

we love
a little

father you built the lines I travel on
my direction was laid by your sweat and death

glitter magpie
take my soul and squeeze it
set your beak and tear it out

eyes of joy
dispel the mist

a hawk in the railway yard
I saw it snatch a prey

peck a hole in the sky
let the magpie through

boats sail cities on secret canals

what is chosen
remains

Guy Fawkes

dragons disperse tonight
like split mercury
amongst the houses

children crouch
round an alley fire

make rings
with glowing sticks

black face michael
hides in the doorway
took the top off a manhole
stretched across two bits
of well chewed gum
and peered down

his jumper sparkles
with drizzle

Alchemist

my attic full of machinery
like spines of the world

carefully shaped brass
and steel spun rich as silk

fine instruments
for exact measurements

soft metallic moan
short anguished hoot
black soul in the tyne

I manufacture ice
my beard scorched white

a solid ball of polished gold

clank of iron on steel track
dogs bark in a back lane

Gateshead

sea monsters chalked on the asphalt floor
stride the alley
as though it were a long cave

we sit halfway up the pyramid to our back door
sun swallowed in the dragon's flame

mammal bodies swim beneath the flapping clouds
which women hang in zigzag lines across the lane

there are beasts with wings in the cellar
beaked and mucky faces contemplate each other

the children have built a toad-run
we sit and watch the sun down

there is nothing else
to do

Jungle

in this jungle
each clump of grass
conceals the dragon
in this clearing
I find a skin

a thin slice
of unending earth
moves at my feet

a broken wooden hut
where the black snake lives
waits for me
beneath the car
uncurls itself between the wheels

San Francisco Snake Dream

the skull masks
          my children wear
are nearer here

          fog horns
     sound so clear
          in this still place

lights burst in the city like illuminated seeds

          siren screams
               re-echo
          through the streets

broke
my daughter's dream
and mine

a snake
with thrashing head

passed on to my son

we ended
chopping it
to bits

Snake Dawn

a blackbird
sang
the sun

raised
towards it
balanced on my waist

she woke
we kissed
I've been bitten by the snake
my tongue
hissed

Storm

surrounded by horses
heads shaking and rearing

I hold her small tit

there is no way past
legs thrash

Next Door's Bairn

waking at four to your cries
        I've grown to expect you
with wall-shaking trucks

that simple cry of need

awake hungry
        your heart opens
and is filled

through thin walls
        when television
and working noises cease
        I count your howls

rain shuttles in the gutter

bairn   a singing star
        quivering lark
over the roofs and slate drains

walls
and the need to break them

I feel your weight
        suspended in my arms
your calls soothe and settle

        awake and cry
my ears are tuned
        and murmurs satisfy

                thrush of tires on the street

        you howl
my typewriter snaps a beat

others hear us
through windows and walls of strange rooms
they tap their feet
some even move their lips
and speak

sing on and scream
I'll stay awake
and we'll assume the shadows
in their dreams

The Gift

the total of everything
is nothing
please take this gift
shadow of the poplar
on the red brick opposite

embryo
how you slip through
no shape
no name
no time to

the child I wept the child
another came
her hair was white
we had been
in each other's dreams

how we build and fall and run

money
if you take all
take none

American Chant

soft bed of cloud
green lights implode
like an angel down
        with wings burning
down
we dip
telephones
        taxicabs

red
    leap on a lawn
on a balcony
    snow sleet
        shadow
in the chandeliers
        american accents
            accidents
born
burning
a suitcase
without handles
out on the slipway
        sleeping
sensual nosecones
nudging nothing
        is this on the run
harbours hard
    highways are endless
cities are savage
    savage
stopping we stultify
    shouting we shudder
        shudder
a boat on your shoulder

In a room of mirrors—
a broken glass.

We dance.
What instrument are you?

A flash bulb
every three seconds.

Your hand on my knee.
My tongue in your ear.

If we whisper
they can hear.

City Song

an engine's echo
              clatters through the streets

bud of a rose
              in my room overnight
opened
           before my mind
took account of time

drunks puke
    through iron gates

the call of bonny girls
        whose echoes giggle
after gifts of love
        from shadows
who share their loneliness
           to taste
their naked bliss

night machine
   and few survive

fierce tenderness

            dawn arrives
drawn in chains

denies flight to sleep

            and none can sleep in flight

except
         a being
                     born in darkness
               whose heartbeats
                  sound like feet
               fluttering
                  from foetus to wreath

a single rose
   which withers
by the bed
      bears joy and grief
and speaks of self deceit

            unwilling watchman
   my ears pierce each sound

flock of sea gulls
   in a narrow cobbled street

            who could release a woman
         or dream there was a key?

her movements are her own
and from the shadows
an ecstatic moan

the city's turquoise mist
is scent of roses

summer sounds
are ceaseless

D

simplicity
say sleep

or
shall we
shower

have an apple

you are
as I need
water

shall I move
do you dream
shallow snow

flesh

melt this

1976
from *The Jarrow March*

Setting Out

A Crusader holds the hand of a small boy
        who walks alongside.

Next to him a woman carries a smaller child
        in her arms.

The bairn imprints the memory
        of a firm grip
on his father's palm.

With his mother
        they will walk to the town's border.

A banner rises above.
        The fluttering wings
of their strength and love.

To H.H. Bishop of Durham

shaking off damp sleep
        in a deserted church
three years deep in deconsecrated dust
        scrubbed clean of holiness
god no longer lives here

a dull dawn through decaying columns
        morning stoves lit on gravestones
a small flame gives warmth
        against your chilled indifference

they breakfast well
        in hell's kitchen

cobwebs obscure the windows
        a pulpit damp
rat shat and rotten
        crumbles in the hand
and is forgotten

here is an organ which once sung
            distilled the rank air
with its leather lungs
            traces of its decorations glitter
cherubs angels piped a holy lilt
            rust neglect decay
all serve to dull disguise
            deny its gilt

David Riley

David Riley stands upon a small platform
            beneath the banner:
JARROW CRUSADE
            in letters larger than a man's head.
The characters are made from their bodies.
The words are printed on the sky.
His arm is raised and says:
                I will not be broken!
His mouth is open and says:
                I will not be stopped!
His shoulders are straight and say:
                We shall not bend!
His eyes are wide and say:
                We shall not close!
His legs are firm and say:
                We shall not buckle!
His feet are steady and say:
                We shall not tire!

A small boy beneath him,
                hand on hip,
a mask lifted from his face,
                him, he too, he says so.

Portrait of a Crusader

cap off
>   a spotted bandana
round his neck

he mingles in the crowded street
>   his badge
his rolled cape across his chest

who are these men
>   from the north
grey faced and clear eyed?

family men
>   hunger dancers

Body Warmth

>   her body by my side
>   gives the warmth of two voices
>   raised in the joy of many

>   rain on the window
>   and the clatter of hopeful tongues

>   sunday 24th of february 1929
>   trafalgar square
>   all flags are red

>   mrs despard   then 85
>   is helped forward

'outbursts of cheering roll like thunder
>   as they recognize
the frail white-haired veteran'

she unfolds a small green flag

"IRELAND WELCOMES THE HUNGER MARCHERS"

54

Hero Dust

"Love is the highway to the door"—Robert Creeley

saw the gypsy lady
told me all bad news
said am goin on a journey
to the land of the blues

saw the gypsy lady
said cross my palm with blood
I'll tell you 'bout your future
an it don't look good

1
an aztec tunnel
    under
the new urban motorway

    full moon
above the victorian workingclass houses

    a doll's arm
under partly demolished terraces

2
rusted wheels
    cast iron cogs
chains poised taut
        abandoned to rain
to sleet
    the memory of trimmers

a southern vessel nudges wooden staithes
    awaits trucks
shunted and unbuckled by teamers

    moss mottled with oil
and slime
    bedding for skeletons of scuttled boats
collapsed jetties

3

     played dominoes tonight
put down the wrong one and won
     threw the I Ching and got "grace"
(it embarrassed Confucius)
     I'm confused

4

     you threw me a glance and a rose
talked of riding through woods on a bike
     sent me a postcard of a russian sun-god
   and a peasant girl in ferns

5

a maze of streets
     and back lanes

four in the morning
       walking

cities reach unbroken
       to the sea

6

men climb ladders
     descend pits
erect scaffolding
     demolish buildings
devise plans
     revise maps

     sun streams through birch
spokes of your wheels alight

7

a cat howls
I dream of you

8

a gypsy surrounded by bairns
    she asks me to fuck

we are over-looked

9

this street is built with bricks
    of furrowed brows
whole gutters explode
    and tremble with sparrows

10

you may not find me kind
    love has no hold on me

hold me

11

earth and a mutual glitter

12

to taste your lips
    I won't smoke
for a month

13

at thirteen I failed to become
    a complete teddyboy
owing to my mother's dark memories
    of Mosley mobs
she did not buy me a black shirt

14

fingers through forests

    you come

a flower
    shakes off its
pollen

    each limb
trembles

15

it's cold
    I crawl up
and curl on you

16

this is the fifth night
    without sleep
I'm bruised with love

17

rats are chipping
    at the skirting board
birds are singing

    it's dawn
    I had to write a poem

18

    hello pain
we meet again
    lovely as before
and strange

    hello sorrow
no need to borrow bliss
    my lips lit
with your first kiss

    why joy
am I your boy?
    your latest toy?

19

play any game
choose the hardest pitch

dance on pain
keep sorrow in the ditch

20

I'm fierce
I'm furious
my fury flames furnaces
my fire flights hawks
my savage smiles ravage hyenas
my dreams devise daggers
demand death

my lascivious laugh

21

oh in she rushed
    flushed
with stolen roses

22

    barefoot on broken glass
shattered mirror

this side of reflection
    chandeliers explode
walls become walls within walls

follow this maze;
    this way out
    is that way in

"Withershins:
    a direction contrary to the course
of the sun"

23

your beak breaks
    the flesh of my breast

I scream
tormented by dreams

24

moon
     full on the sea
what waves there are
what tides

     your eyes
wide
as a mother's thighs

25

a hot animal lies beneath my hand
her ribs take the weight of my fingers

she wears her scar like a jewel

26

I hear her whine in the wheels of a diesel
     her body the aroma of nipped buds

27

in unlit Boilerhouse Road
   an astronaut on a moped passed me
I hid in Reservation Street

"you are lost in the maze of a dying culture"

she too had joined the cavalry
     I replied

it dies in your betraying eyes

28

     "I have saved the bird in my breast"

death's eye
     smiles with the mouth of a flower

Northern Line

a ten-year-old boy
        with glasses
and scraggy
           red hair
keeps falling off
    to sleep

he counts
        the cooling ovens
they're all around
        a forest
  of smoking towers

by him
    a white bag
with blue letters
LEEDS UNITED
      and in gold
THE CHAMPIONS

is that your team?

aye!
      who'd you support
  newcastle?
    I don't suppose you
want to talk about
    last saturday!

I didn't

Cream of the Scum

It's in the net.
    Not quite, pet.
Hero.   Puddin.
    You stupid gett.
What a good'n.

It's off his heed.
        It's in.   It's not.
He lacked speed.
        What a farce.
Next time use ya arse.

It slipped off his boot
        like a greased rat
up a drainpipe.

Hero.   Guttersnipe.
        Cream of the scum.
With a heed like that
        you should be hung.

> *lovers lovers*
> *football brothers*
> *rejects dejects*
> *clowns and crakaz*
> *boot im one*
> *in the nakaz*

He's on the floor.
        Not any more.
Get it back.
        Give him a crack.
Lob it.   Stop it.
        Put the block on it.

Watch ya teeth his elbow's lethal.
        He's trying. He's tripped.
He's flying.
        Did you see him shift?
I'll buy him.

> *Lovers lovers football brothers*
> *Rejects, dejects clowns and crakaz*
> *Boot im one, in the nakaz.*

White Rose

you gave me a white rose
        put the lamp on the stove
        it caught fire
the I CHING said
    "thunder above the lake"
lightning in Baker Street

switched on the cooker
    and blew a fuse
        blue flash
you see
        the whole experience
    is electric

Snowflake

snowflake
    my kisses fall
on your warm
    neck
in a storm

Rat Palace

I got into trouble from the Labour Party
for saying the unemployed man did not have
the intelligence of a dog—when a dog is
hungry it takes its food . . . steals it . . .
                    (P Scullion, Organiser Jarrow March)

"Inmate: One who dwells with others in the same house" (OED)

        the ears are closed
snapped off and blocked
death behind the eyes

how can we help each other?

some lives can't be lived
it's time to assume a more
rational perspective

every word is meant to be read

they punctured both his ears
    and someone died

let's put a hat on all this
and head for home

where?

                    *

I gave a girl an atlas
and since they took away
my passport
        it's only a book

squires of the global village
give us prizes and prisons
the telephone is tapped
outside my window I hear
a disembodied short-wave radio

the guard dogs in Brixton are better fed
than the inmates

30 per cent of prison staff in Wandsworth
are badge-wearing members of the National Front

tax the dole   build more cells

they are looking for volunteers to
collect the shit parcels

I'm not one

these laws are meant to break us

*"some of the children were buried alive
and as they thawed
the earth moved like a field of corn
when they suffocated
the earth was still again"*

E

Ballad

bird chase bird
    across a sky
we'll make love
    when leaves turn dry

bird chase bird
    through tall trees
we'll make love
    where earth bleeds

bird chase bird
    across sand
we'll make love
    in no-man's land

bird chase bird
    on mountain sides
we'll make love
    where water divides

bird chase bird
    beneath a fern
we'll make love
    beside a burn

bird chase bird
    through burning grass
we'll make love
    and dance and laugh

bird chase bird
    from dawn to dusk
we'll make love
    till love makes us

Trick: Fancy Resistance

shakespeare's
birthday

many happy returns
early morning
wolves bark and
            howl

spring winds
race through
cages

what do tigers
dream of?

I wish you could see
your face
when you panic

roy rogers sings
oh give me a home
where the buffalo
and the deer
and the antelopes

you sleep with a dictionary
for a pillow

I am mrs tex
ritter

it's the real thing

I have a moon
in every pane
of my window

that's why you all smile so much
you eat so well

Restless

City Garden

in a city garden
she took me to her side
now
no other place
can I abide

round a city wall
we walked
saw names of men
and women
chalked
and flowers
marked their fall

in a city garden
she took me to her side
now
no other place
can I abide

Jewish Cemetery, Warsaw

I walked in a wood
which did not sing
and a songless silence
hung deaf in my ears

the dead grew roots
held their bones tight
tree smashed packed earth apart
growing higher than the murder camps
higher than the smoke from living flesh

the dead here will never rest
their fingers rattle
in the wood's twig twisted top
where two solitary hooded crows
have built a nest

I walked in a wood
which did not sing
and a songless silence
hung deaf in my ears

Gypsy Music in Krakow

sitting in an alcove
    on the old
city walls
    a three foot
gypsy musician
    plays a violin

his left leg
    dangles
over his right
    and
his feet hang
    far
from the ground

he sings
    with a cigarette
in his mouth
    broken lines
which compliment
    the strings

his half blind eyes
    flicker
like butterflies in spring

magnificent music
    issues from
    the dwarf's
misshapen frame

we stop
        and listen
amazed to witness
        such easy skill
from so
        improbable
a source

a woman
        fresh from church
rushes to push
        pennies in his purse
as she might
        with trepidation
kiss the foot
        of the baby christ

if he appeared
        with such a
moustache

Détente

a city in your smile
    a continent on this tongue
an ocean on those lips

two falcons grasp a single branch
and flowers mouth their way through soil

the sun is out
and draws you through my pores
like sweat

I throw your picture down
and turn away depressed
return annoyed
confused

I want to run my lips
    along your neck

I found a hole in my heart
and fell into it
there my children play
and make a zamek of my wounds
each day

another shape
a heart complete
grows beside the first
begins to drown the other
with its thirst

I stood between my two hearts
and both were beating

a swallow flew into this room
and banged against the window
I caught her in my hand
and felt her heart pelt against my palm

we were both held
her wide swift wings
in my anxious grasp

I wish to tell you about my prison

my fingers are the wings of god
his crushing love rushes through
their veins

it's blood that makes us love

Poems don't get written without poets getting a lot of help. There are many kinds of help which different kinds of people can give. To quote the old Negro chain-gang song:

"Money thinks ahm dead."

But I have been blessed with good friends, and I take this opportunity to thank them.

Particular thanks to Eric Mottram who made the present selection and to Basil Bunting for his invaluable advice and ongoing support.